CW01468146

shedkm 1997 - 2005

designed & published in liverpool UK by shedkm ltd dec 2005 - printed in barcelona by bookprint SL dec 2005
© **shedkm** 2005 all rights reserved   ISBN 0-9551924-0-4 & 978-0-9551924-0-1

this new 'blue book' celebrates shedkm's eighth year in practice by compiling a series of images of projects completed, plus a glimpse of what is to come. using a simple full page photo format interspersed with drawings and quotations, the book attempts to encapsulate visually the difficult to define ethos which drives the studio. shedkm is known as an innovative UK architectural practice with much of its work being in the housing sector, but there is another side to this young team which is very particular. enthusiasm for modern architecture has been a top priority for the studio since its formation in the summer of 1997 - shedkm has always professed modernism as being the appropriate design philosophy for the 21st century (this after many years of neo classicism and contextual vernacular having been the prevalent form in the UK). their approach therefore attempts to be clear and direct based on the belief that architecture should be simple and unambiguous and able to live easily in most situations (including conservation sensitive areas). the projects illustrated demonstrate this: for example the collegiate and the matchworks were completed in grade II listed shells - both winning major awards. oak farm, another winner, converts a tudor farmhouse. the corbin house is built in the south derbyshire green belt. other examples of this ability to combine old and new include southport pier, fort dunlop and lister mills. nevertheless, as well as this apparent specialisation, shedkm's portfolio of newbuild has consistently grown. the blue hotel, ashfield HQ, moho, the vanilla factory (which inserts an exposed structure into a sensitive inner city conservation zone), 'farmhouse' which uses a modern framework despite its name... new initiatives in leeds are unashameably contemporary. arguably shedkm's studio ethos can be most clearly illustrated in their choice of field trip destinations - corbusier's marseille unité, alsop's big blue, la tourette, vitra, botta, herzog de meuron etc. this time the story is in picture format, but next year a 'red book' of drawings will be undertaken - to be ready for 2007.

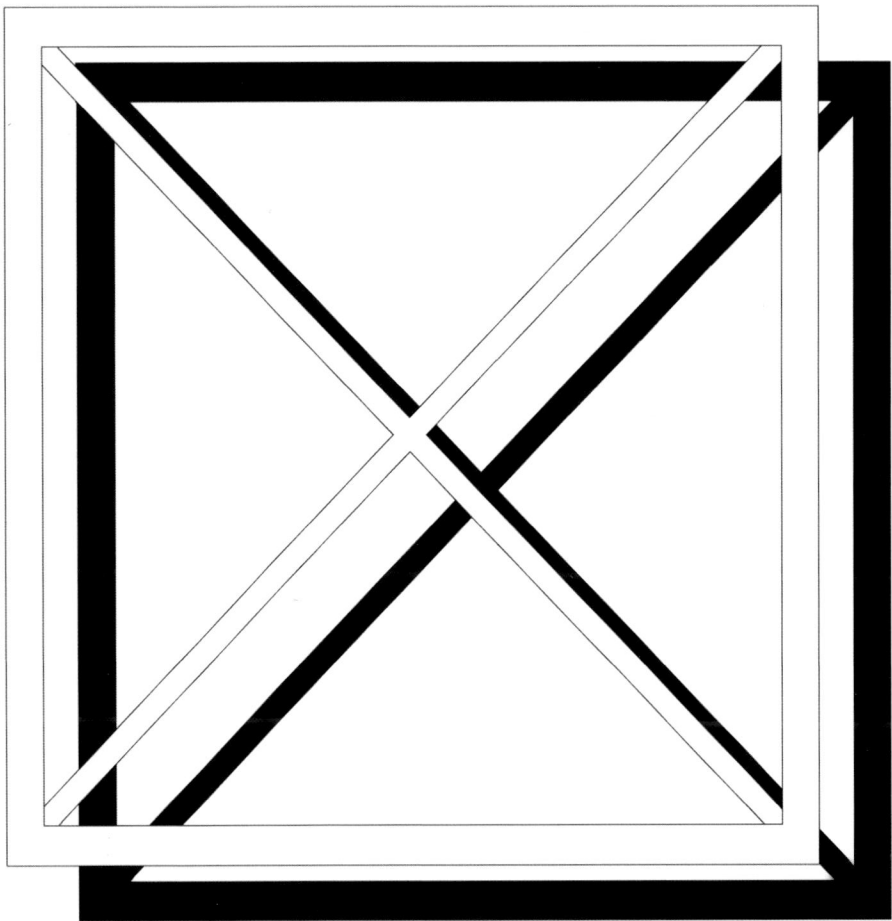

'ineluctable modality of the visible, at least that if no more...'

james joyce - ulysses

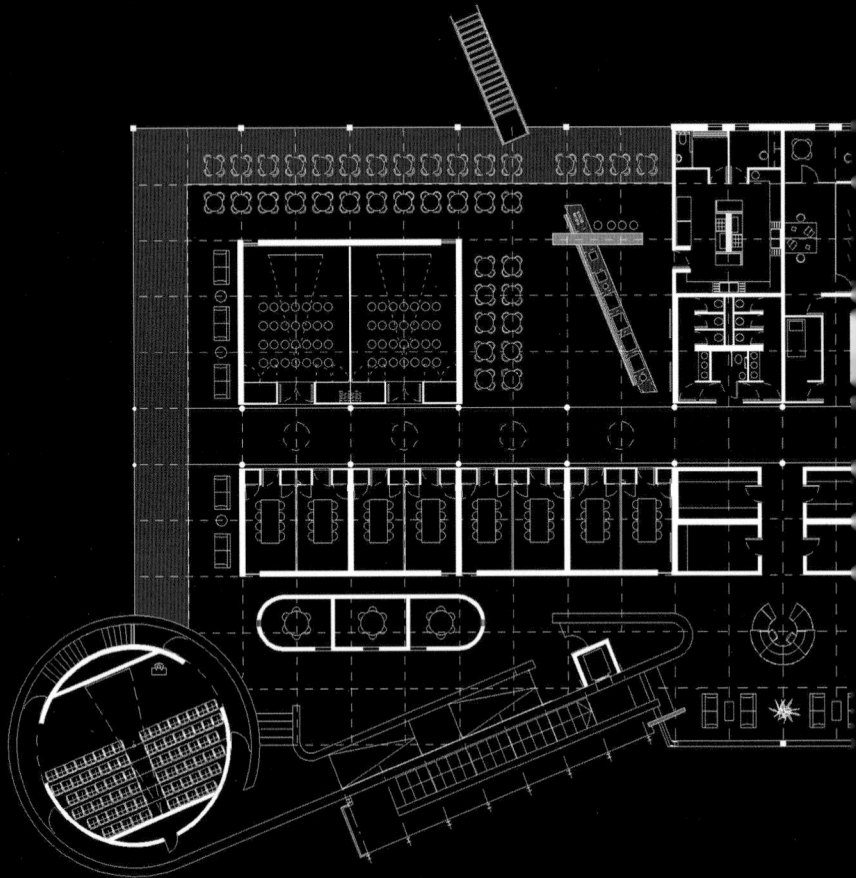

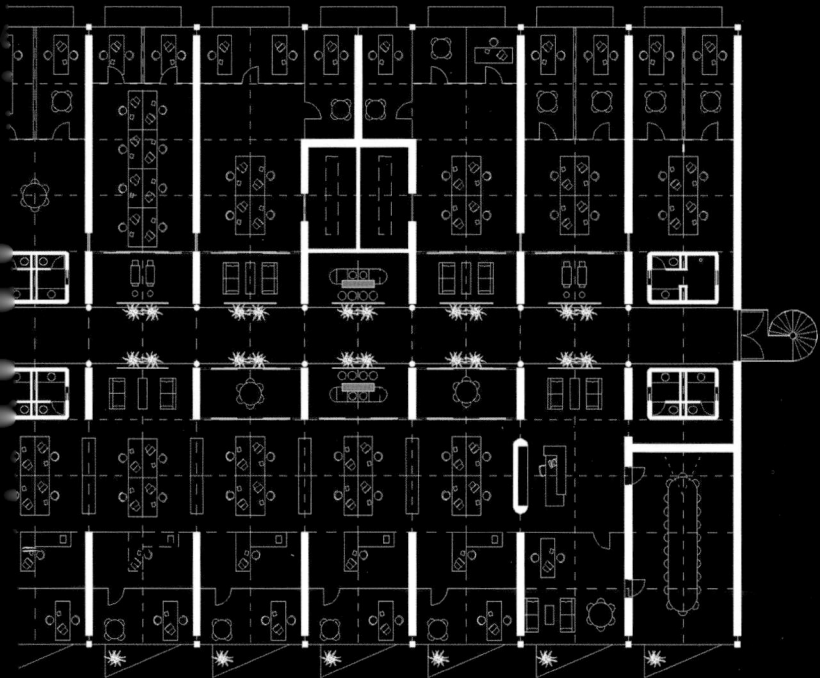

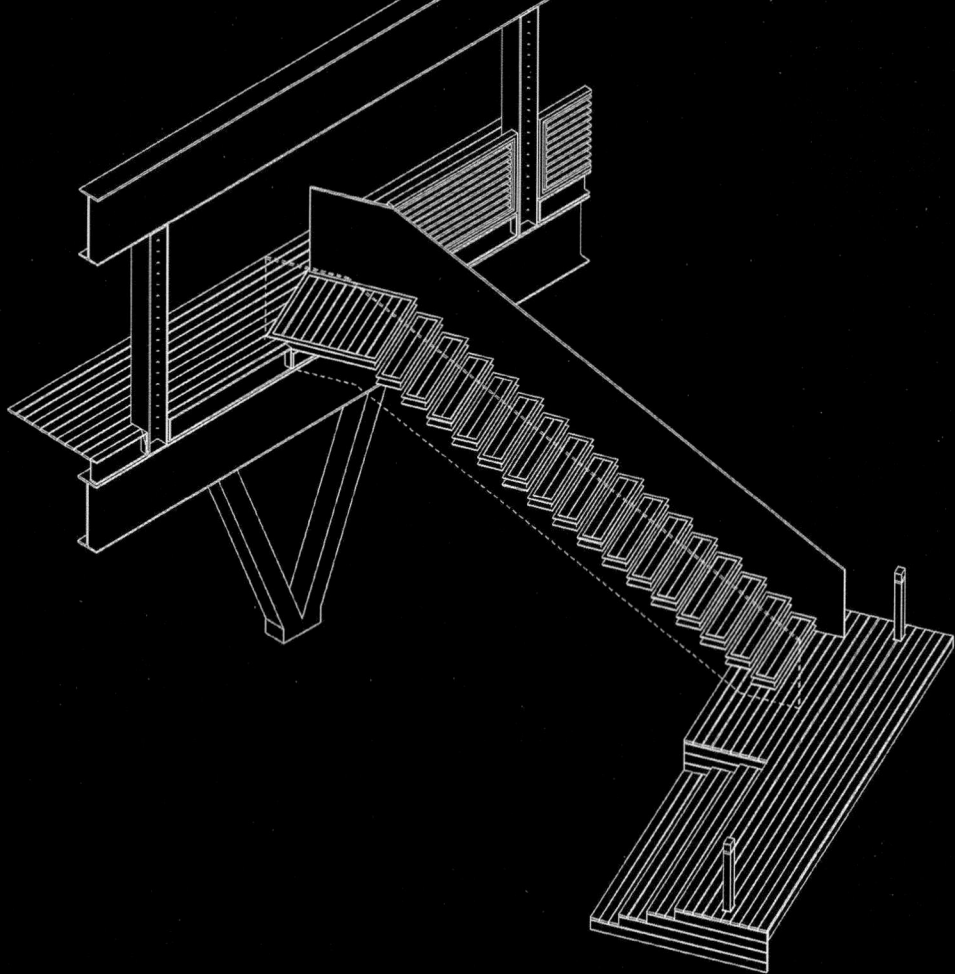

'it is an amazing success story, which started with 4 people working from a back bedroom 6 years ago...'

chris corbin - ashfield healthacare

'maybe it is a good thing for us to keep a few dreams of a house that we shall live in later....'

gaston bachelard - the poetics of space

'the palace hotel at fort romper was painted a light blue, a shade that is on the legs of a heron, causing the bird to declare its position against any background'

stephen crane - the blue hotel

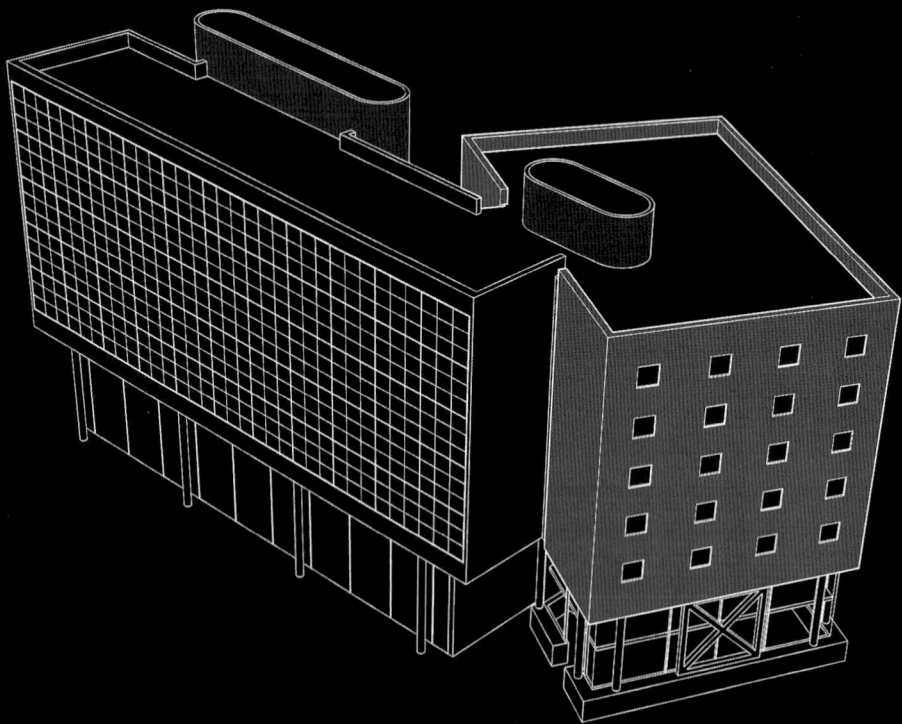

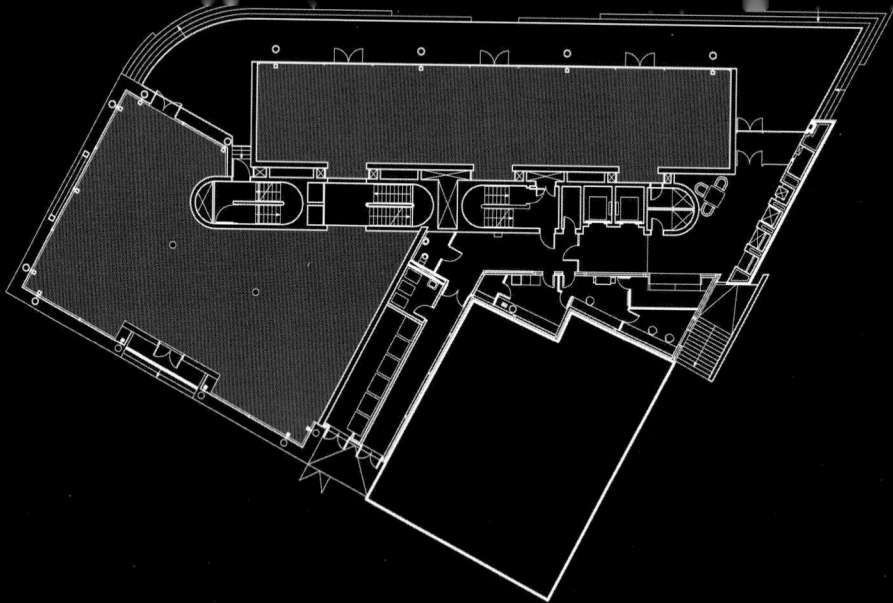

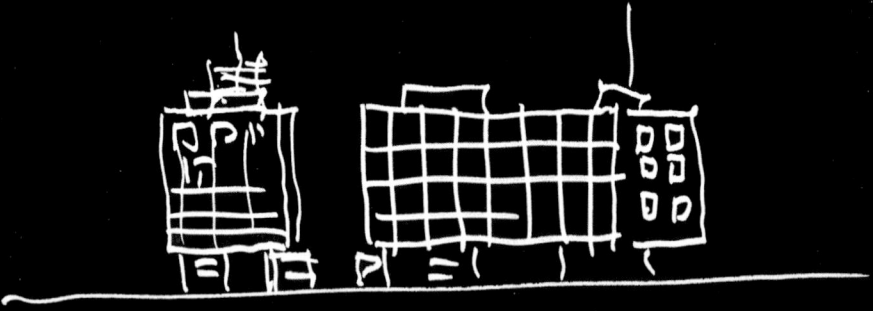

'in the gardens and homes designed by me, I have always endeavoured to allow for the interior placid murmur of silence...'

luis barragan - pritzker prize acceptance speech

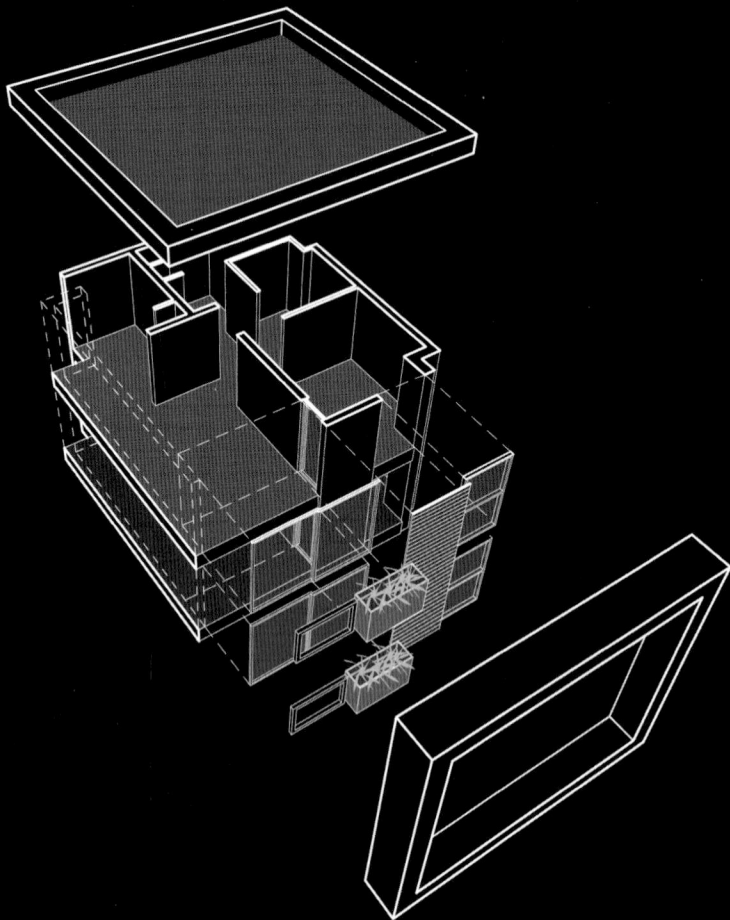

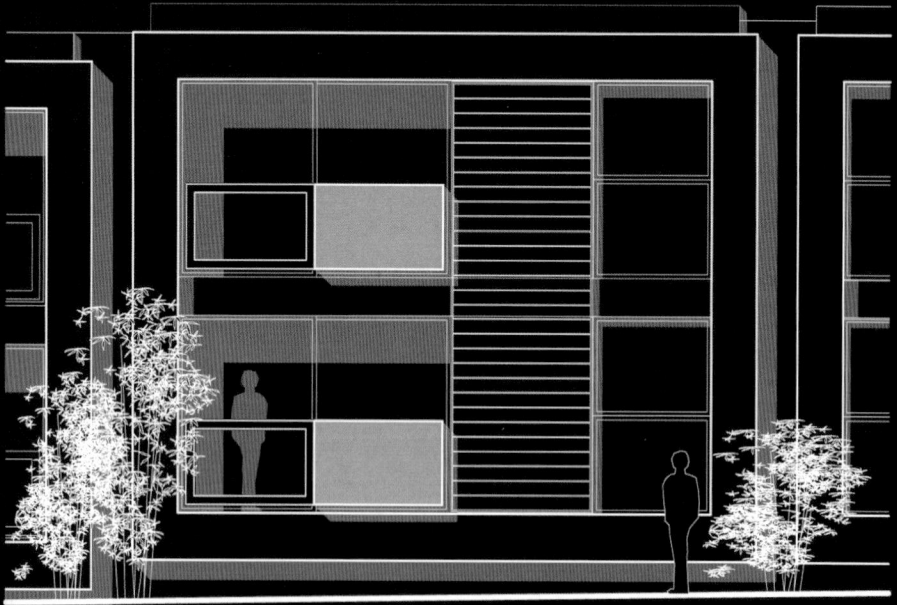

harvey lonsdale elmes architect (1814 - 1847)

Don Solfe Enge us Vir tus Alt ar Virtutis

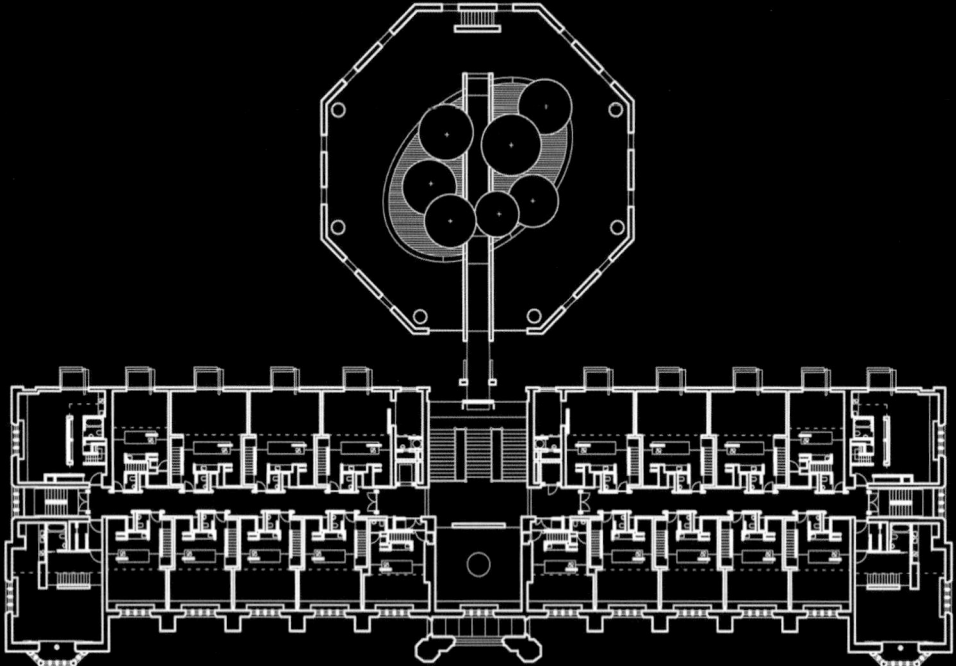

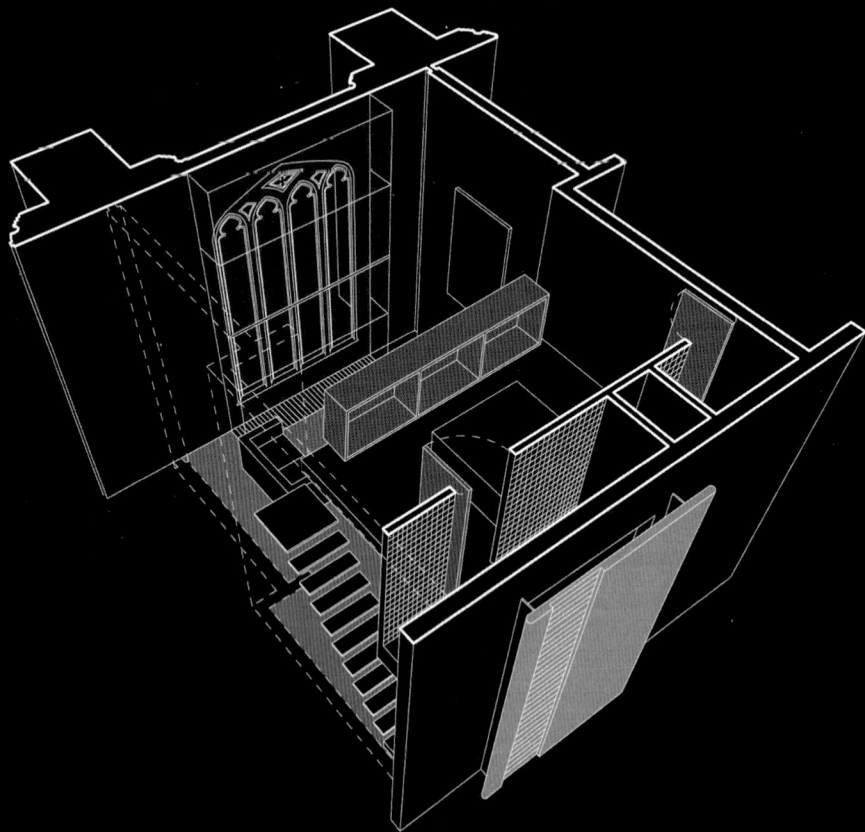

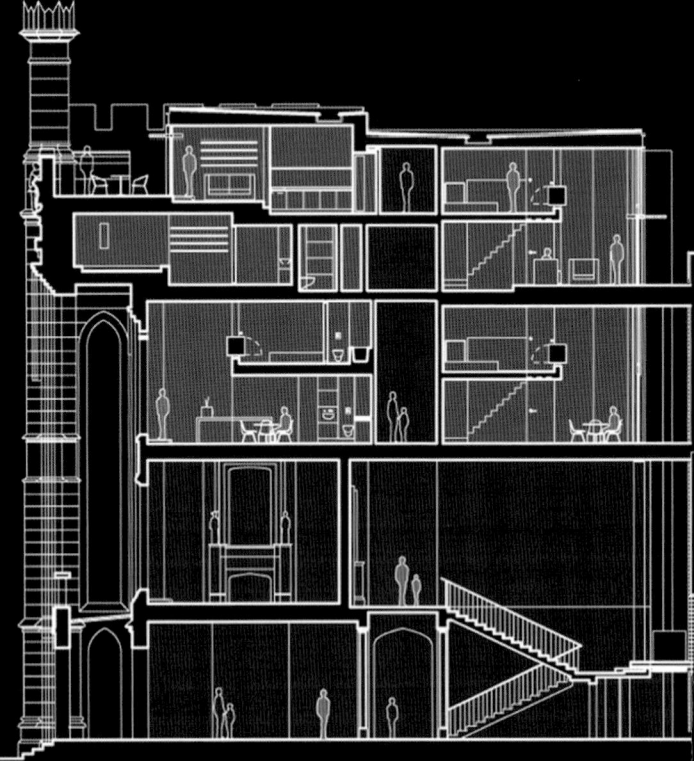

'sometimes the house of the future is better built, lighter and larger than all the houses of the past...'

gaston bachelard - the poetics of space

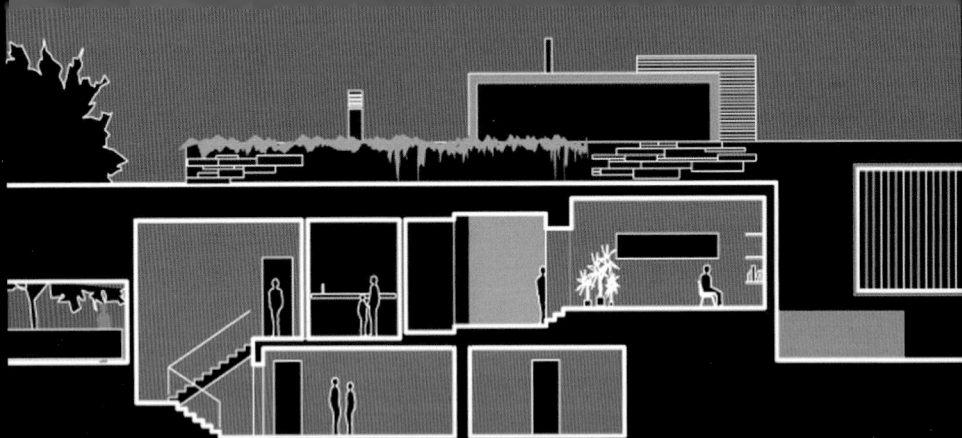

'a house that was final... would lead to thoughts -
serious thoughts - and not to dreams....'

gaston bachelard - the poetics of space

*'the village was a little surprised - to say the least,
by the manner of this intervention...'*

oxton resident - 2004

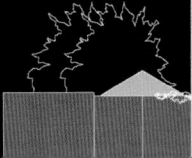

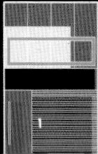

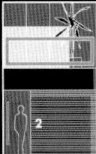

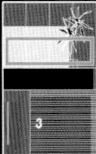

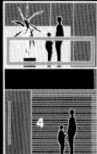

' remember - it doesn't matter what you choose to do, so long as you make sure you do it extremely well...'

tom bloxham - flaine 2002

GRANDS VANS

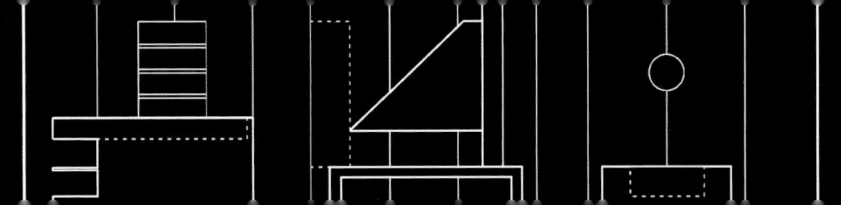

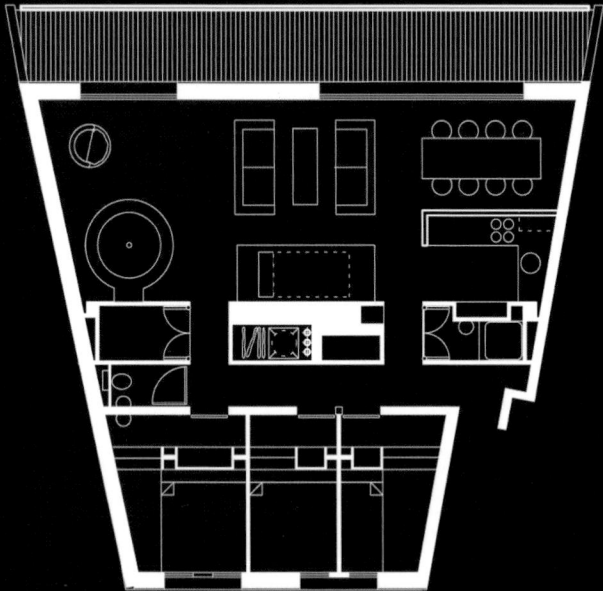

'hope springs eternal... even in the face of adversity'

alexander pope - essays on man

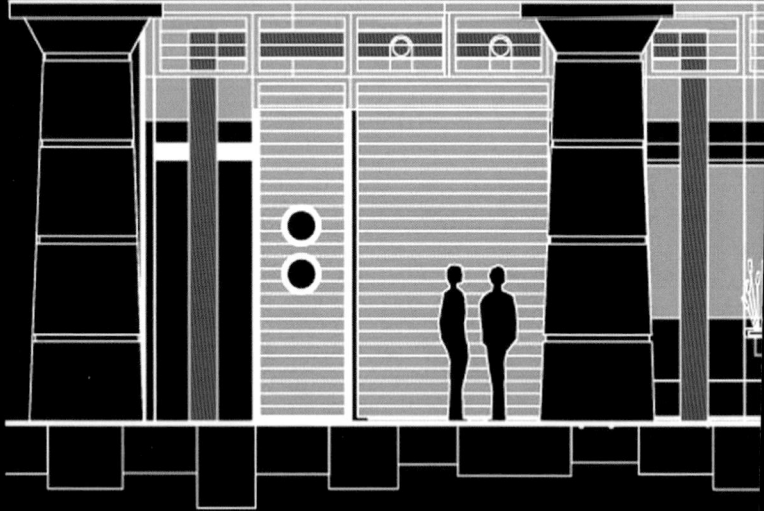

...be on the waterfront

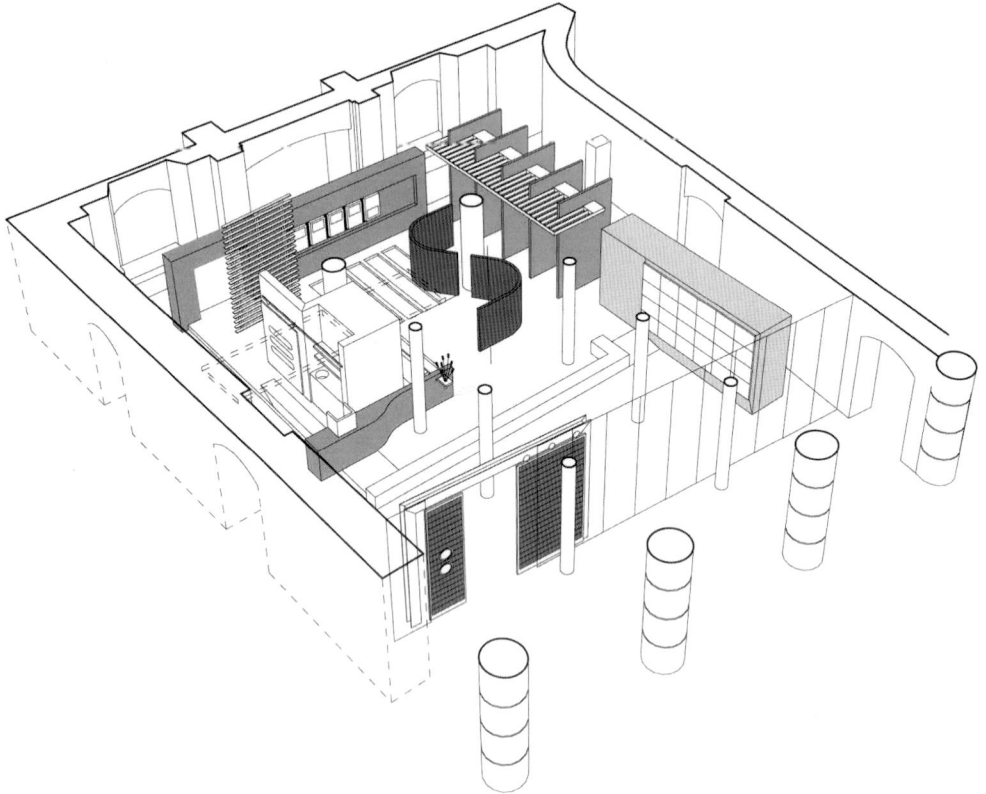

WELCOME TO HOPE ON THE WATERFRONT

'some aspects of colour in general and red and black in particular...'

donald judd retrospective · tate gallery 2004

the matchworks

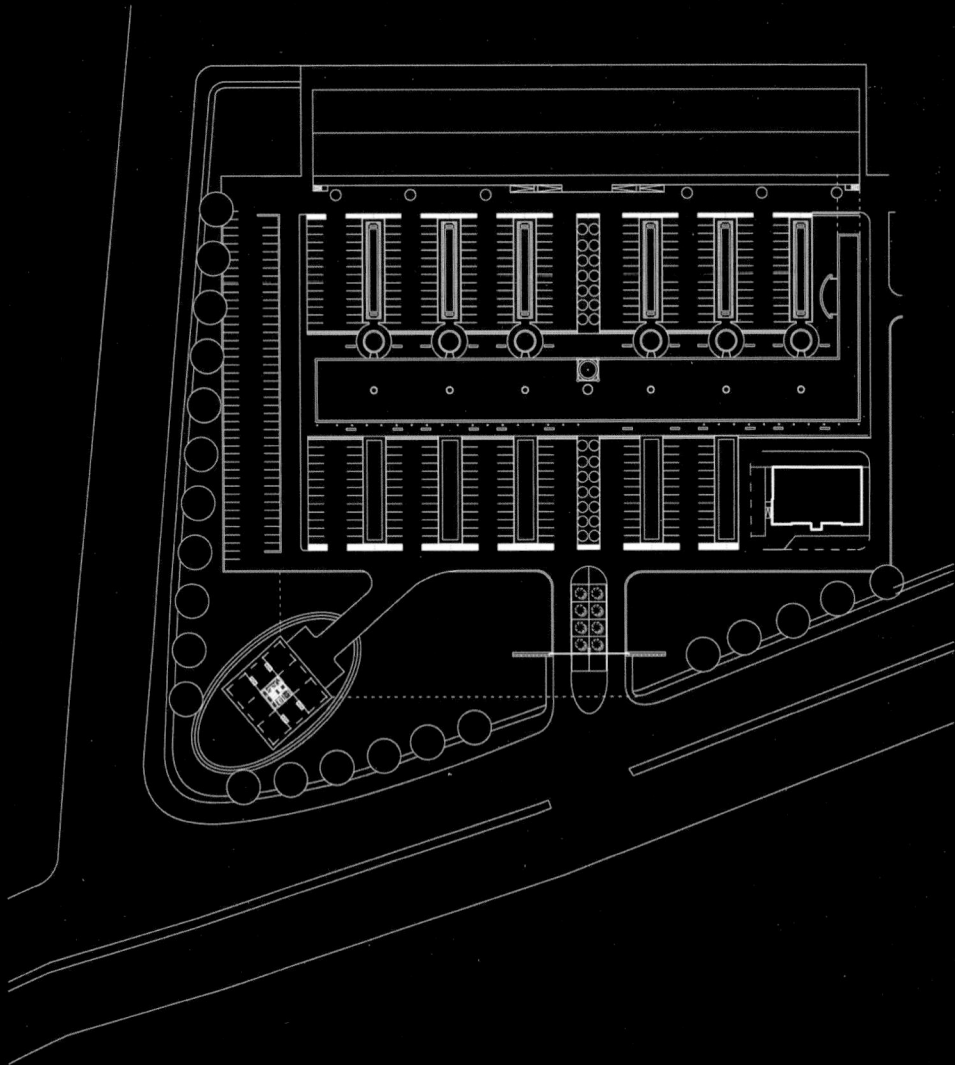

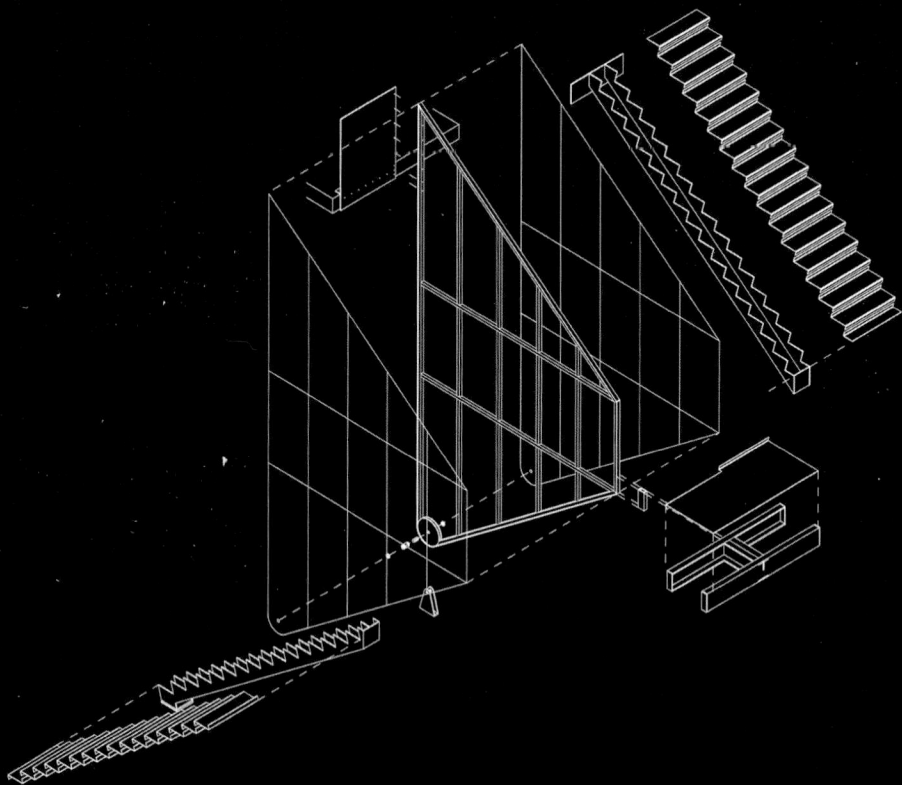

'what motivates my enthusiasm for architecture when it's basically such a long hard slog to achieve anything of quality - is an unconditional passion for it...'

james weston - 'football and me' building design journal

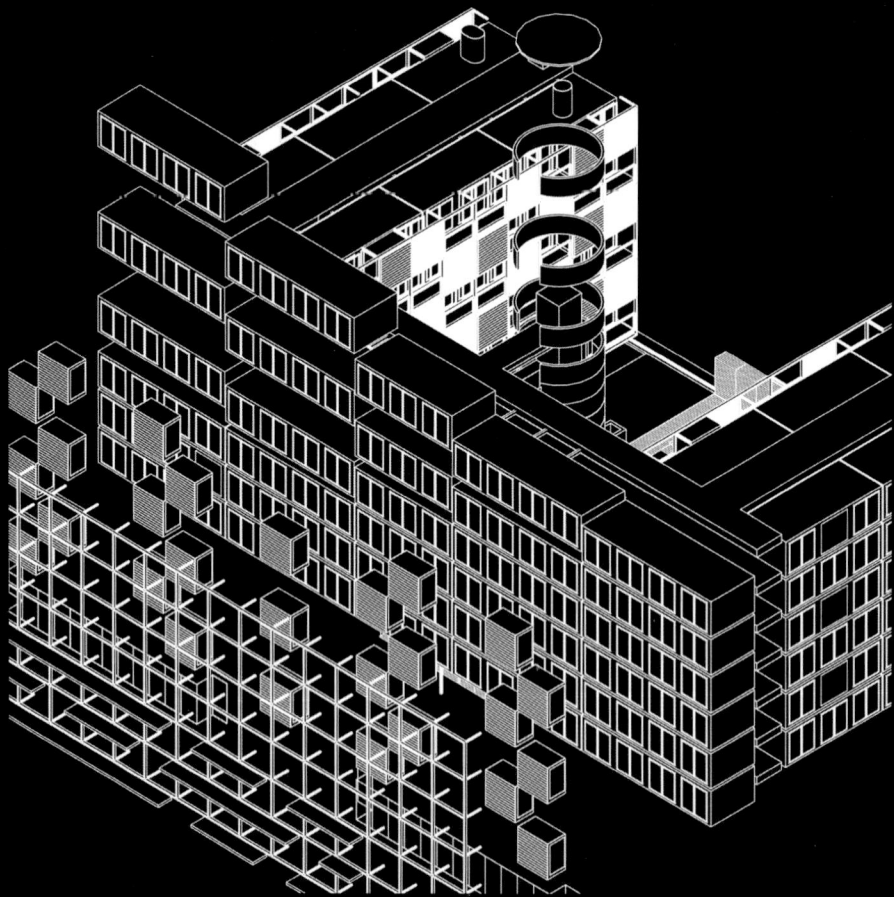

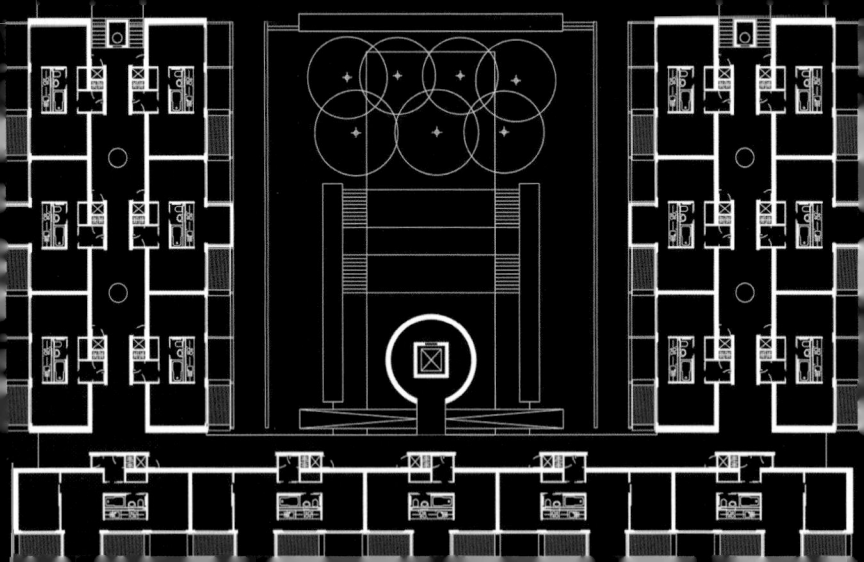

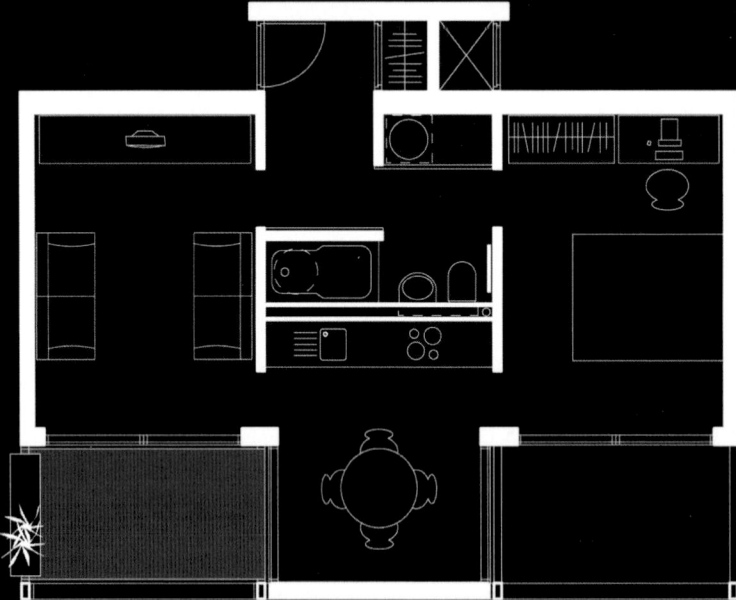

'special care should be taken - if you build, not to go beyond reasonable limits in costliness and splendour'

cicero 106 - 43 BC

'a tree is an image of a complete construction'

le corbusier

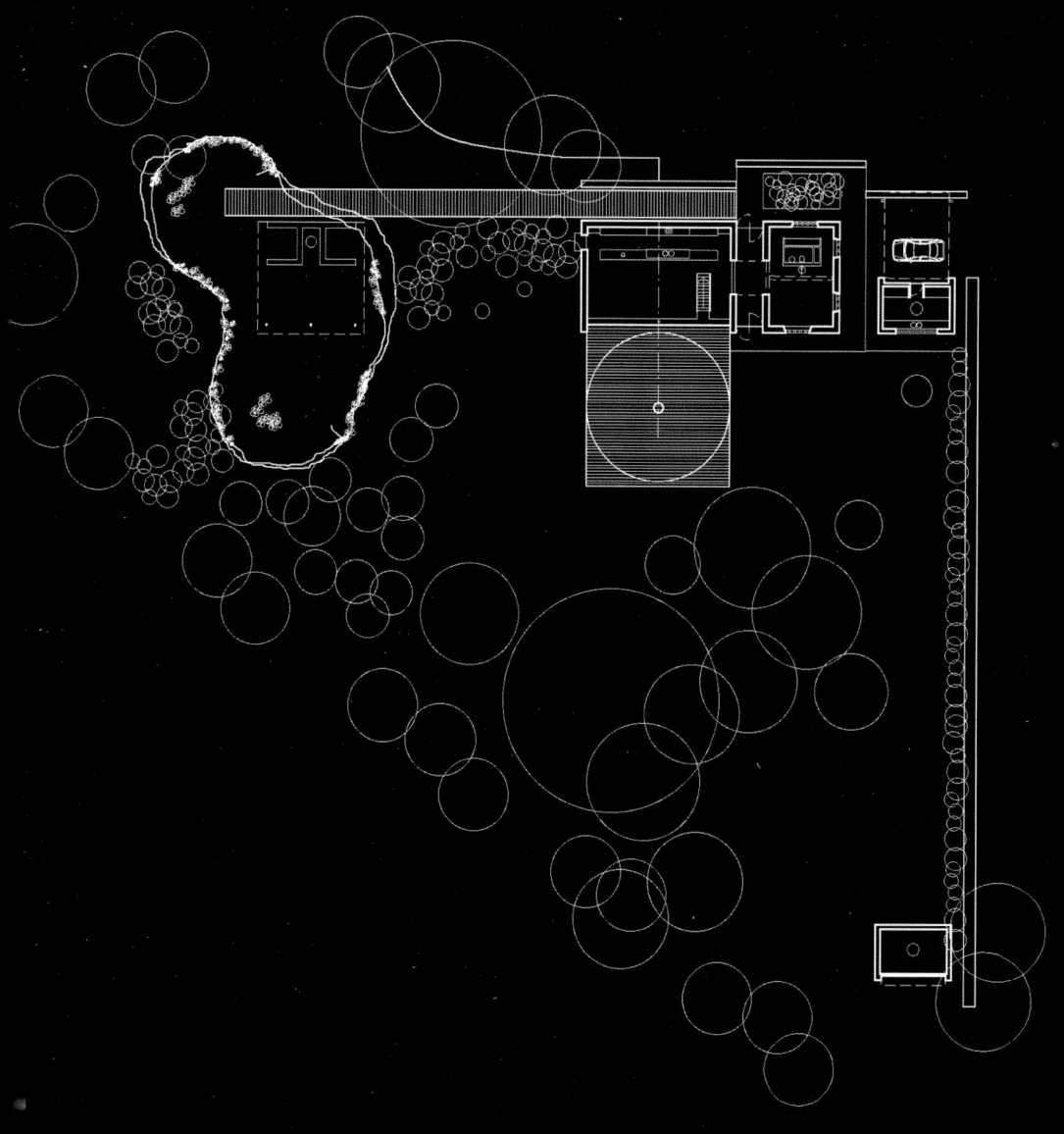

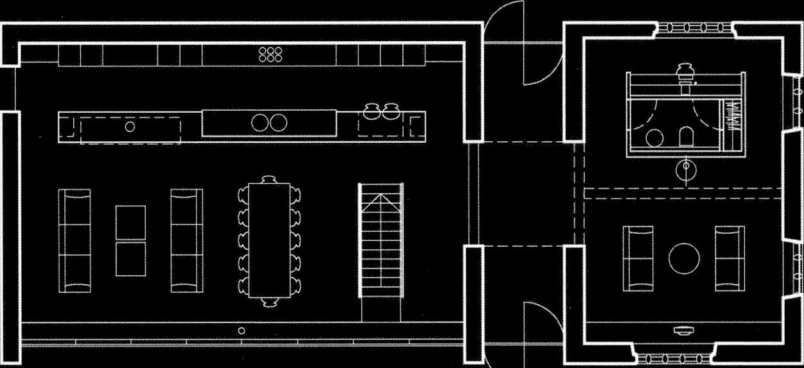

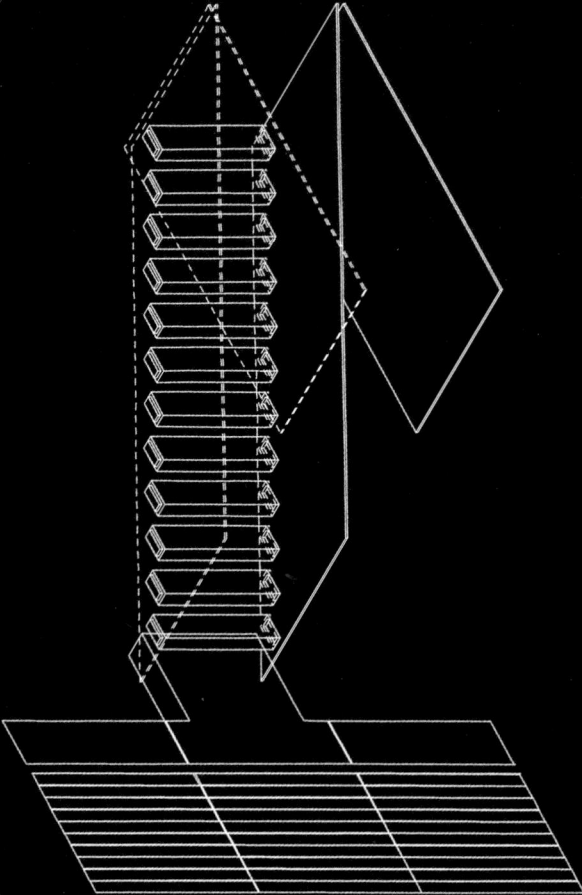

'it is also the house of emptiness, for it is free of all ornament, except what little is necessary to satisfy the aesthetic aspiration of the moment...'

okakura kakuzo - the book of tea

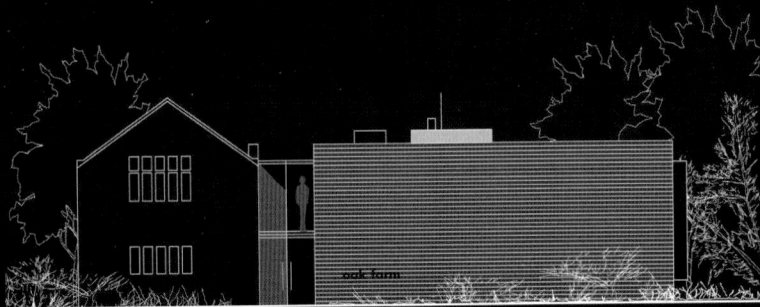

'and some small detail is always left unfinished to be completed by the play of the imagination...'

okakuro kakuzo - the book of tea

'the city displays one face to the traveller arriving overland, and a different one to him who arrives by sea...'

italo calvino - invisible cities

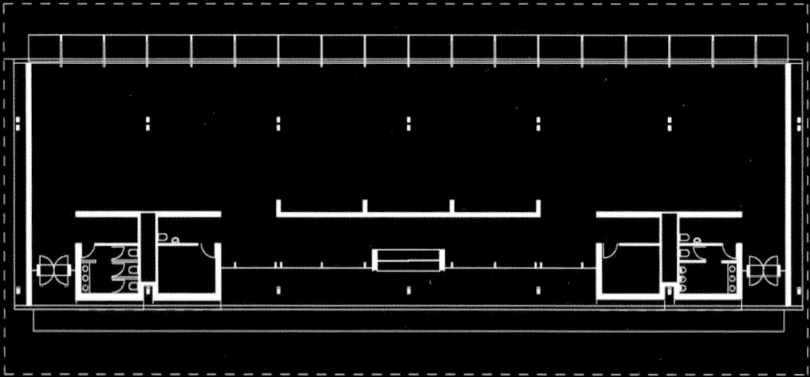

'...conjuring modern affordable dwellings from a difficult landlocked site is a model example of urban regeneration...'

housing design awards 2000

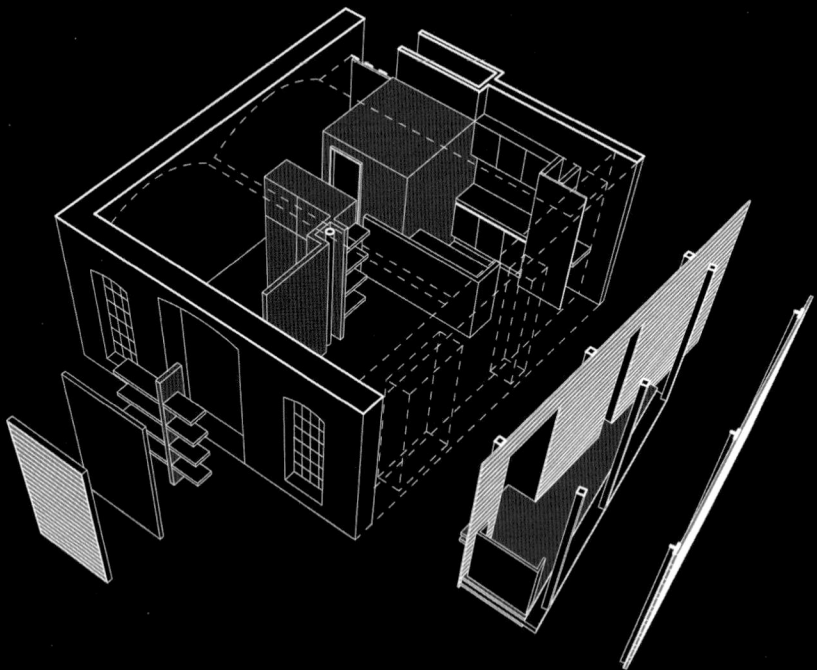

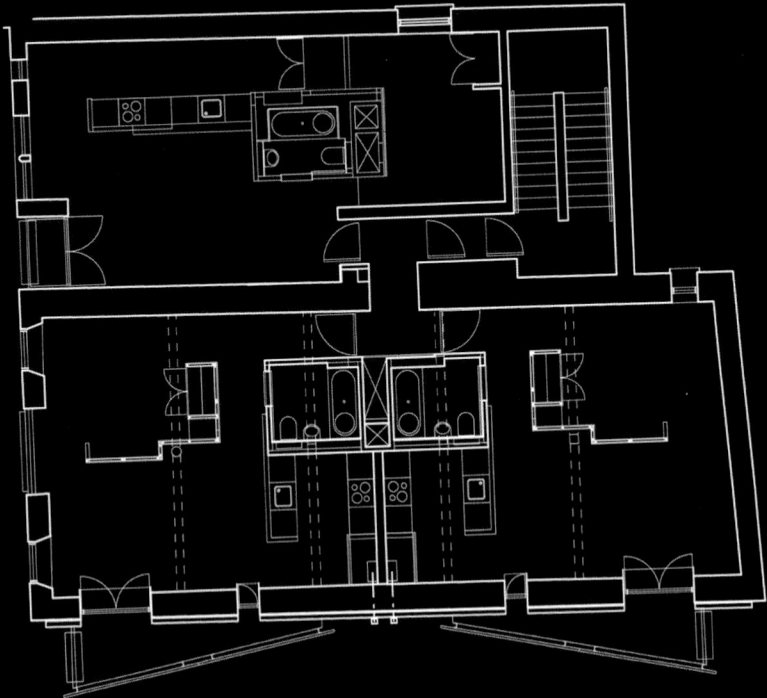

'its absolutely awesome.....'

guy jackson - urban splash

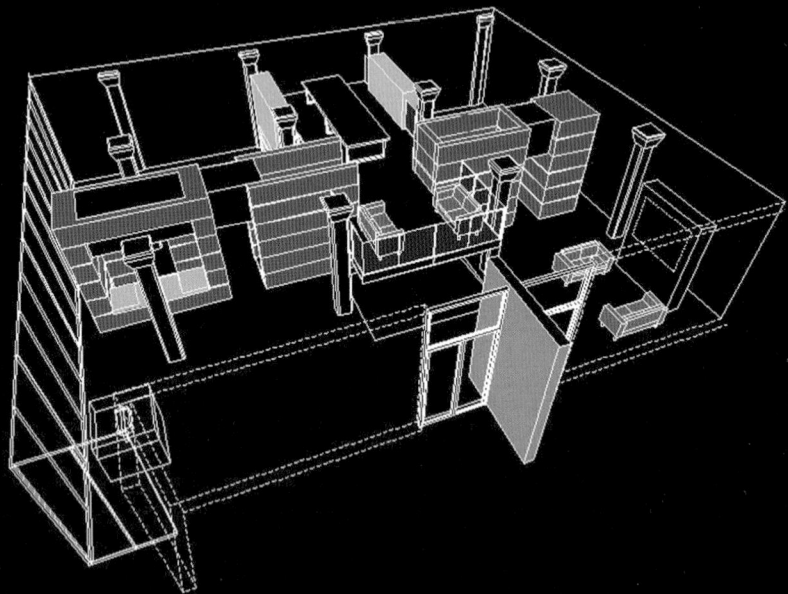

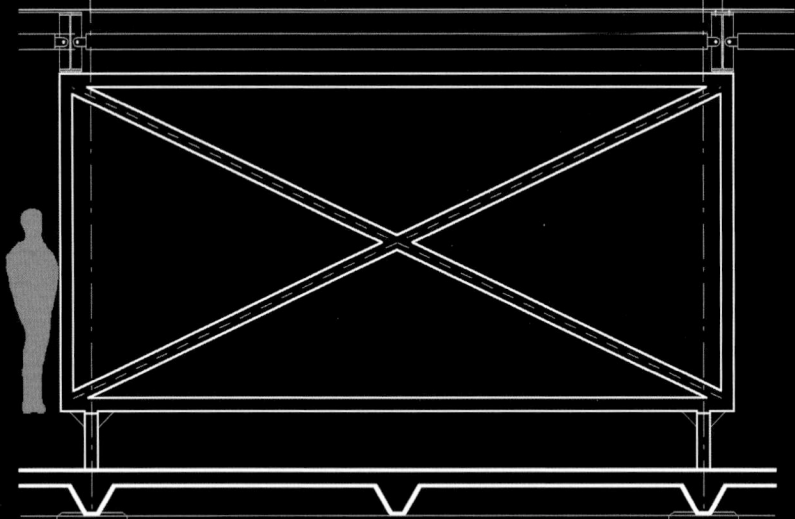

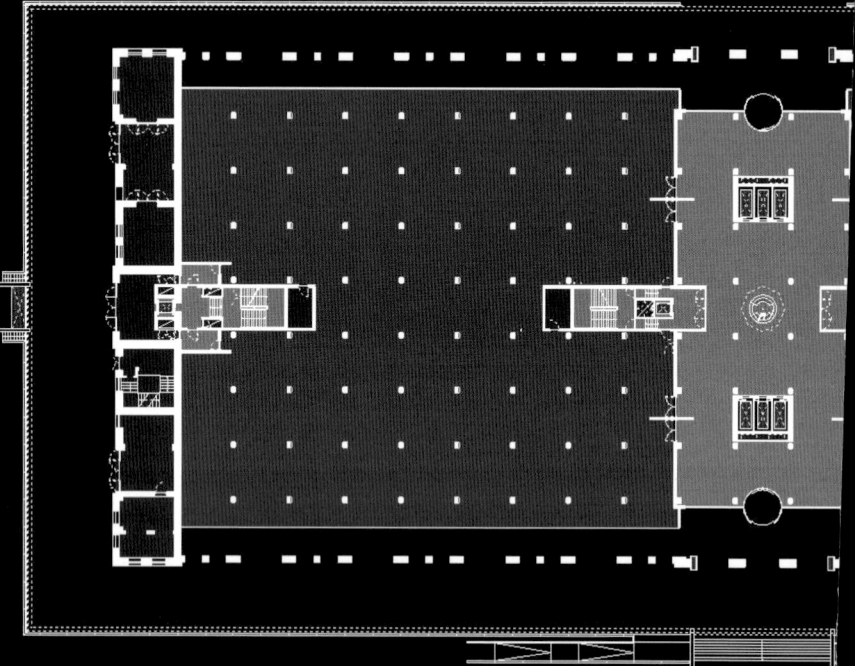

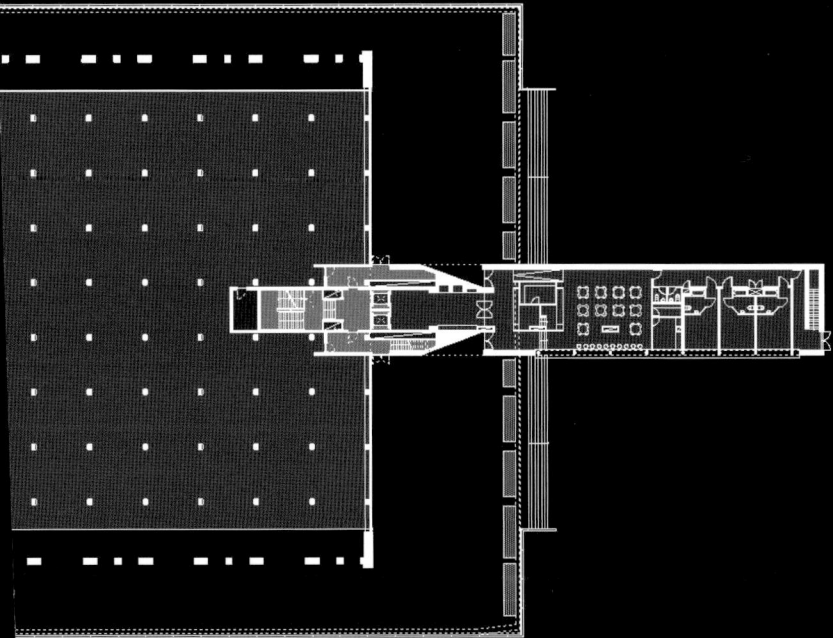

'I don't care what it costs, I don't care what scandal it causes, I don't care how long it takes, but that's what I want...'

jorn utzon (the saga of sydney opera house - peter murray)

'designing is a journey. you set off to find out - to learn.
you accept the unexpected.... you don't hide, you go on.'

renzo piano - logbook

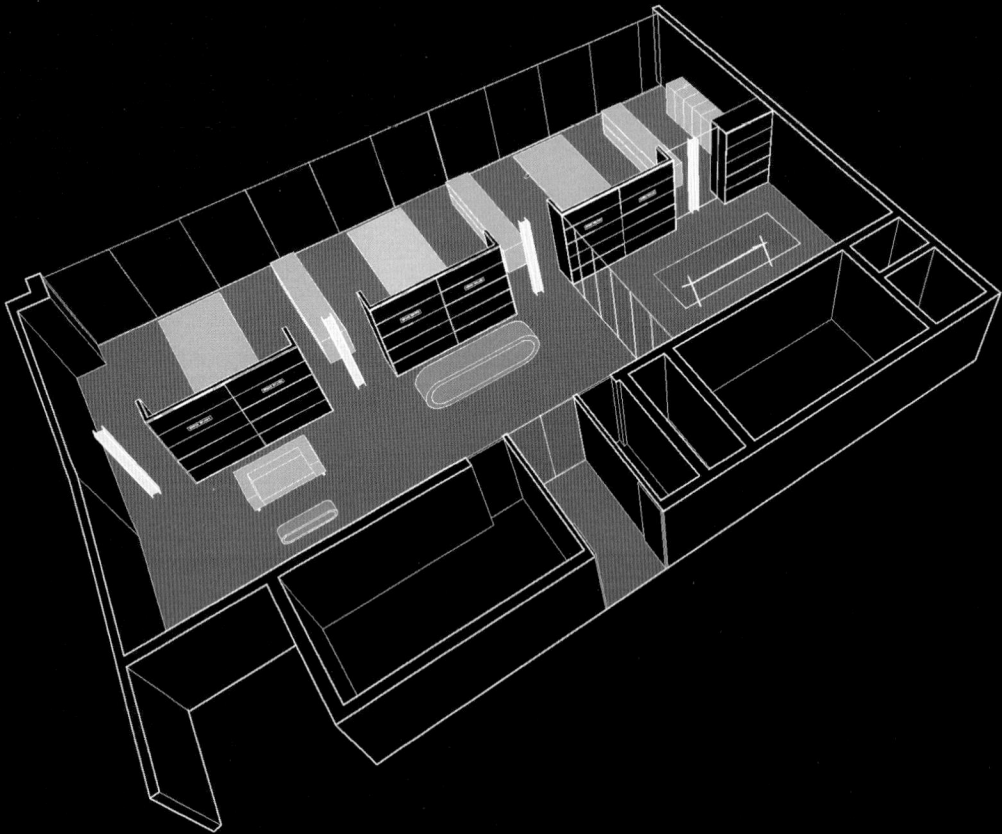

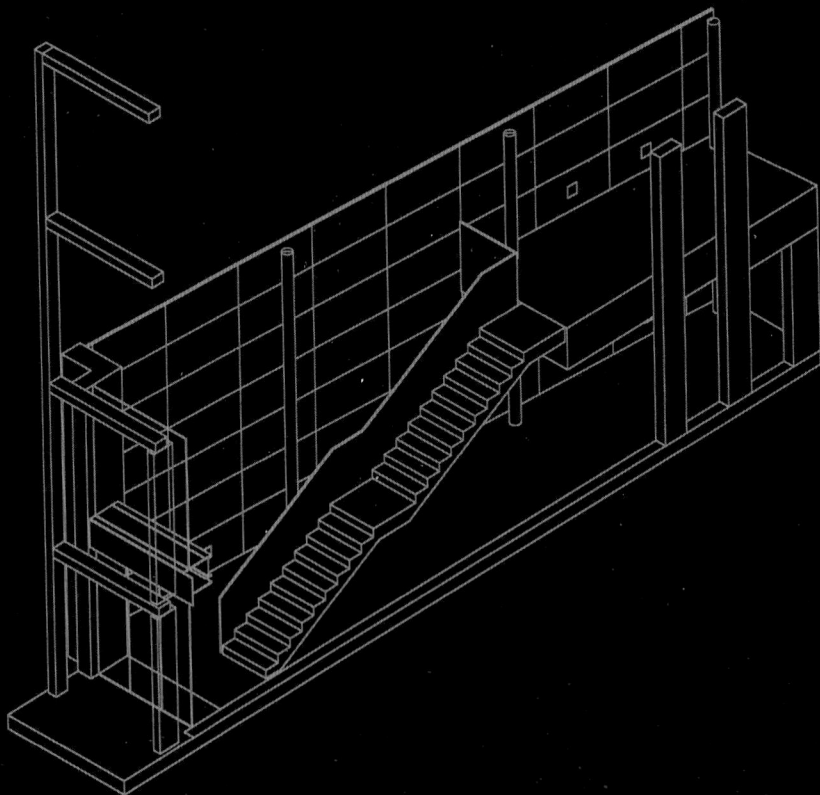

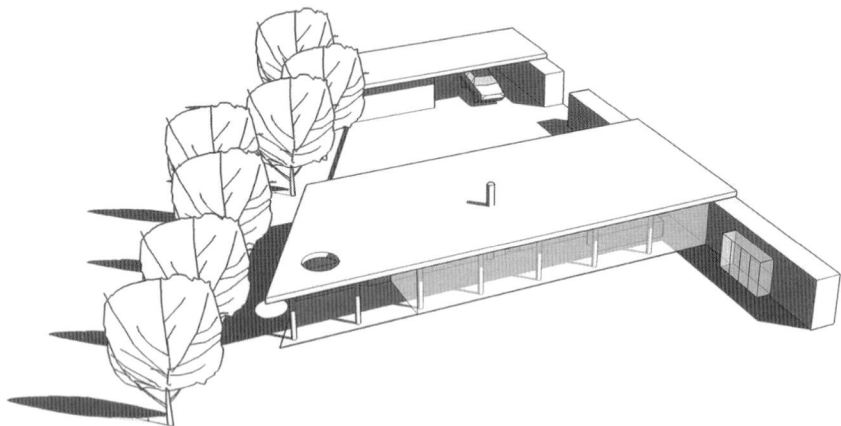

ashfield - the ashfield healthcare HQ at ashby de la zouch was designed for a limited competition in 2000 and completed 2 years later. a long low open plan building suspended over 100 car parking spaces echoes the ethos of this vibrant training and marketing company, operating exclusively for the pharmaceutical industry. white steel, glass & concrete contrast with an italian marble drum shaped lecture theatre. a lively internal boulevard complements ashfield's youthful ethos

the 'blue hotel' - a short story by stephen crane inspired shedkm to use yves klein blue in an abstract form for this city centre travelodge budget hotel. it is to the credit of city planners that such an idea could be realised in the midst of a conservation area which now enjoys UNESCO status. a tight site, 104 bedrooms, street level commercial units and a fast design & build contract. sharp detail & strong colour give the travelodge brand a new aesthetic impetus

care village - one of the liverpool housing action trust's final projects is a care village occupied by long term tenants from ashgrange in knotty ash. shedkm's international competition winning solution (1st phase completed 2003), combines an internal street with generous apartments on two levels. an orange drum contains community facilities and links the scheme to two refurbished tower blocks. the design has been widely published and critically complimented

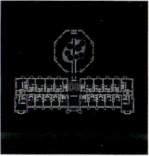

the collegiate - shedkm's first project for developers urban splash involved taking a ruined grade II listed school designed by harvey lonsdale elmes (architect of st george's hall) and inserting 96 'loft' style apartments around a wide double height corridor. the fire damaged octagonal theatre becomes a formal garden, and the neo gothic decorated windows of the main facade stand in front of planar glass internal walls. the design has won RIBA, civic trust & housing design awards

corbin house - this luxury home for chris & sam corbin in etwall derbyshire closely followed the completion of ashfield healthcare (their private company). the design uses long interlocking brick & stone walls and was closely monitored by the local planning authority. corbin house is one of the very few new modern houses that have been recently approved in the greenbelt. a spacious entrance hall leads onto a swimming pool with formal views to the landscaped grounds

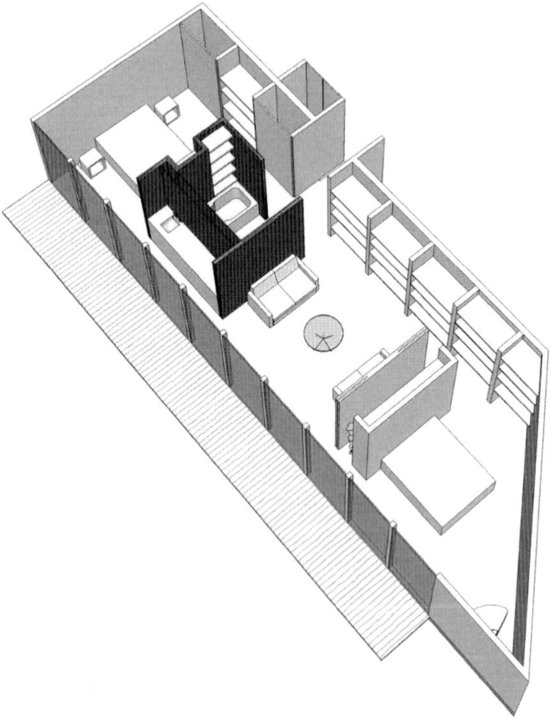

the dyeworks - a typical shedkm small scale development in oxton village birkenhead, the dyeworks scheme integrates four town houses into an old workshop premises. 1st floor living, open plan, exposed trusses & brickwork plus a balcony facade extending the front elevation of the property. the design forms a template for a succession of proposals in the wirral as yet unbuilt. aspects of this project have informed later shedkm schemes - such as langworthy & moho

grands vans - tom & jo bloxham wanted a ski apartment in marcel breuer's flaine complex near geneva - an open wood fire in an ultra modern fireplace was a must. shedkm & swiss architect guido truffer created in an extremely small space an example of bauhaus style continued right through to the household artifacts. in direct contradiction to current alpine ski resort trends, primary colours contrast with cool vals stone, and an internal hot tub shares space with the open fire

hope on the waterfront - conversion of a major space in the albert dock for liverpool hope university posed another fast build logistical challenge for james weston of shedkm. this facility (a combination of cafe & interpretation centre), involved the integration of multi-screen AV technology with grade II conservation problems in liverpool's premier tourist destination. a similar facility was planned for wigan, but hope's strategy of such centres has not as yet been continued

matchworks - another grade II listed building - this time the old bryant & may match factory, evolves into an award winning business complex, again with urban splash. the jury said 'clear geometry reminiscent of the hard minimalism of 1960's artists such as judd, morris & andre...' the matchworks with its abstract formalism epitomises shedkm's design approach. also, the project is an example of how close client/contractor/architect co-operation can deliver award winning quality

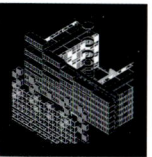

moho manchester - the first of shedkm & urban splash's innovative modular unit designs brings a new degree of sophistication to this typology. the moho starter apartments, built offsite and craned into position, have wide balconies, sliding walls and a contemporary minimal ambience. recently, shedkm have received international interest in the system, so these elegant units hopefully may be seen again - other shedkm/urban splash schemes are also being considered

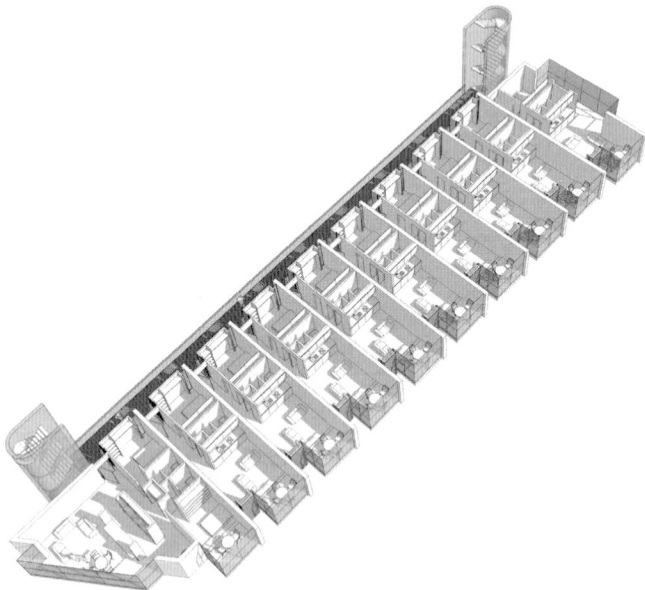

oak farm - jonathan falkingham's home as designed by shedkm is a blend of modernism and electronic wizardry contrasted with the traditional stone of a 15th century farmhouse. the main accommodation is in a 3 sided stone 'box' with a window wall overlooking a wide landscaped garden. the open plan with a long automated food preparation area has the ability to adapt to social and business events - with the farmhouse providing a warm and close family atmosphere

pier pavilion - southport's pier pavilion is situated 1km out to sea, so the job of building the shedkm design (won in a competition) was daunting. however, a combination of clear planning and crisp detailing has helped this NW town to gain 'pier of the year' and other awards - plus much media attention. little more than a precisely controlled and constructed shelter from the storm, the building with its environmental control and stunning sea views, has proved immensely popular

preston point - a derelict warehouse in central liverpool provided a shell for 15 shedkm modernist starter flats for maritime housing association. preston point, with its housing design awards is something of a cult development in the plethora of national housebuilder residential initiatives currently on offer in the city. the original brick arches and open plan living of the lower stories contrast with two small penthouses which have superb views over st george's hall & the museums

the fort - fort dunlop is shedkm's biggest and most long running project to date. the regenerated warehouse occupies a highly visible site alongside the M6 at birmingham making the most of a dramatic concept which uses the extension of a blue services spine into a 7 story hotel with a matrix of porthole windows reminiscent of a transatlantic liner. a highly visible roof deck with conference suites and the building's insignia, completes the illusion. scheduled completion - 2006

vanilla factory - urban splash's liverpool HQ is situated in this development which uses the device of an exposed frame new build 'hub' to link a series of starter offices for the ropewalks creative community in liverpool city centre. the white frame stands clear of the facade, and automatic external sun blinds are used for the first time by shedkm. the vanilla factory with its strong imagery has proved instantly successful and links with a courtyard to the original baa bar pub

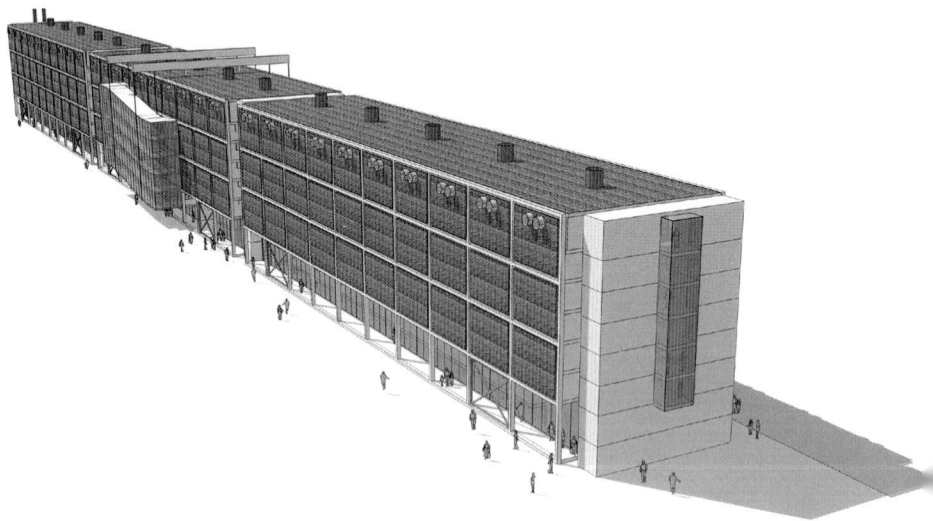

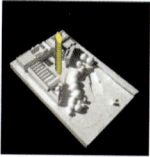

old haymarket - a long running initiative with urban splash has produced a number of schemes for this pivotal city centre site adjacent to the mersey tunnel entrance. the nature of the gap site lends itself to a commercial solution, but currently residential is the preferred option. recently talks with city planners over the possibility of a 30 storey tower have taken place. shedkm's urban design & masterplanning is illustrated in the various solutions proposed for old haymarket

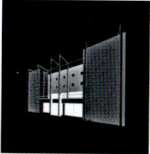

walkabout - one of a series of small to medium size projects that form part of max stone & wendy dixon's development strategy in liverpool's ropewalks. this addition to an australian chain's first liverpool bar, provided an entrance and two access stairs using steel glass & timber. perhaps more of interest to historians, the framework encloses the space that had been intended as a bedroom block for a small boutique hotel. the possibility for such an infill still remains

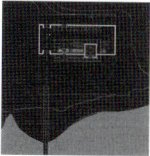

liverpool sailing club - shedkm was approached by members to design a comprehensive scheme for the sailing club to replace vandalised premises on the mersey at speke. the clubhouse would be at first floor level above a boat and car park with a secure boundary. members would be able to follow races and enjoy a dramatic view through a large glass wall (similar to southport pier pavilion). the scheme was not progressed as funding bodies moved the project elsewhere

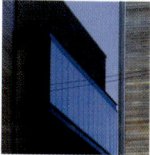

wonderbar - another shell construction forming part of the ropewalks masterplanning exercise for frenson ltd. here a group of warehouses are made useful by (as in walkabout) the addition of external stairs & services cores. the aesthetic is again steel, glass and timber cladding and, as with all shedkm buildings, the detail is careful and precise. also, the way these buildings are occupied can easily change - currently bar & club activities form the main use

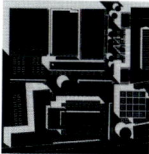

ropewalks - a developing masterplan including walkabout, wonderbar, vanilla factory and shedkm's new studio building. shedkm's approach is to knit together a series of smaller schemes which are tackled over a developing timescale. even schemes which are not on adjacent sites can be linked through familiar detail, materials & aesthetic, with spaces between buildings being utilised and enhanced in an area which has been run down and neglected for over 50 years

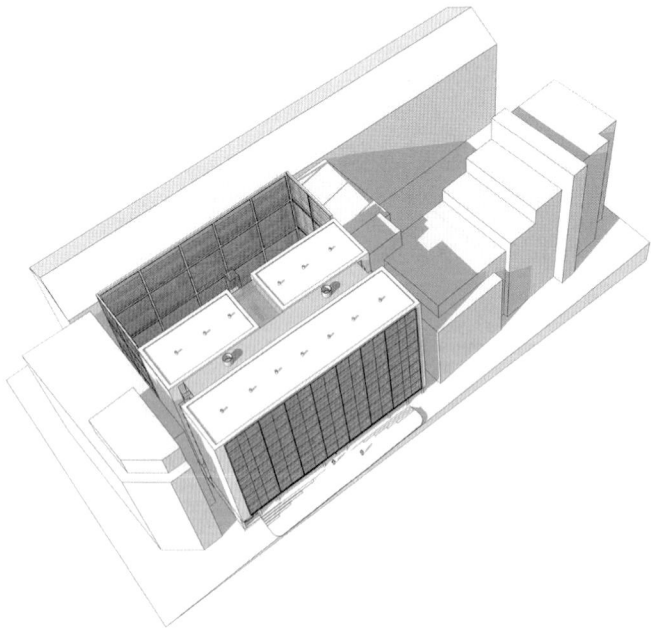

giancarlo ricci - an early shedkm job, the ricci bar was a fast build sophisticated addition to a quality fashion outlet. initially high flying and used as a venue for fashion shows, the starbuck chain assured its eventual commercial success. for shedkm, ricci (designed & built in 3 months) was an object lesson in logistics... a massive rubber clad sliding wall separated the cafe from the shop, and the stainless bar unit was inspired by typical italian espresso bar aesthetic

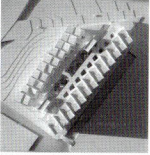

tree house - competition winning scheme by shedkm for 100 eco friendly apartments as part of will alsop's 'masterplan' for new islington east manchester. the tree house was designed in collaboration with taylor woodrow & is currently awaiting statutory permissions. the formula provides two interlinked blocks of duplex accommodation along an open air matrix of walkways through a dense copse of evergreen trees. an alternative to the urban splash/alsop 'chips' block

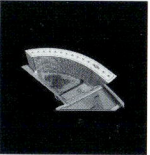

arc (sar) - a speculative scheme for 300 apartments for morris properties close to leeds city centre. the flats are arranged on a curve slightly projecting over the river aire with offices and commercial space occupying the three lower floors. the arc scheme is just one of a series of initiatives for the studio in east yorkshire following their involvement (for urban splash) with the lister mills bradford masterplanning and major landscaping exercise currently in progress

langworthy - a comprehensive regeneration of 396 terraced houses in salford for urban splash (in partnership with salford city council) to provide 1st time buyer affordable housing in a hitherto deprived area. the concept takes the traditional terrace and provides modern 'loft' style living with 1st floor open plan and private patios. this is renewal of coronation street on a grand scale - most certainly shedkm's most socially significant and rewarding project to date - now on site

lister mills - shedkm's masterplan for the famous manningham (lister) mills in bradford, draws on industrial typology to create a series of formal axis & spaces in scale with arguably the most imposing group of mill buildings in the UK. the chimney becomes a massive iconic tower on the crest of the hill with a formal link to lister park 1/2 km away. the perimeter 'wall' is retained, entrance portals mark critical node points, and much use is made of corten steel and industrial artifacts

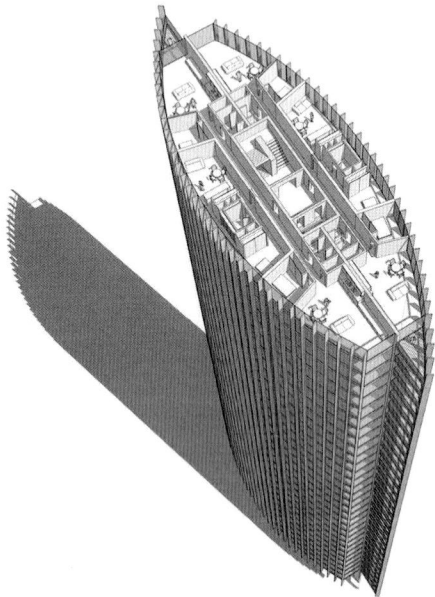

bottle lane shedkm advanced to be one of the last two high profile practices to be considered in a national limited competition. eventually won by benson & forsyth, the final stages which were undertaken under a strict fee structure, took both schemes to a high level of immediate preplanning application detail. this scheme on a very tight site in the centre of nottingham was extremely testing having to accommodate several disparate uses in a commercially viable framework.

bridge house this project in west yorkshire again takes the principles used in runnymede, the corbin house and oak farm (shedkm's award winning design in allerton), and proposes on a smaller scale a site responsive version for a developer client in leeds. in this case a double wall accommodates service elements (as in the corbin house, but privacy behind it is obtained by using the garage element to form a courtyard bounded on its open side by existing trees - due 2005

runnymede a scheme for a private house in caldy (wirral) designed on similar plan principles to the corbin house in south derbyshire. the house was to be raised above the ground and constructed from a steel frame with glass panels behind a wall of local stone. by this method the view towards the river dee and the welsh hills beyond was maximised. the project was designed for a developer, but has not been taken further. an example of a classic modern movement plan

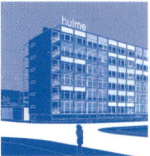

farmhouse a project for 56 family units for R-gen in hulme manchester - the scheme for an ecologically responsible developer (some affordable units are to be administered by a housing association), draws on a traditional plan within a modern fast build framework. for example units will be entered via a large family kitchen used as the living hub - hence the 'farmhouse' logo. the design as approved is scheduled for a planning application to be made in november 2005

littlewoods building a very familiar liverpool landmark, the littlewoods building in edge lane is now saved from demolition by a consortium of northwestern development agencies. the original use was as a printing works for mail order operations, but shedkm's scheme for urban splash indicates 200 living units plus a hotel overlooking the botanical gardens. now a live project for urban splash & shedkm, this iconic building will help mark capital of culture year 2008

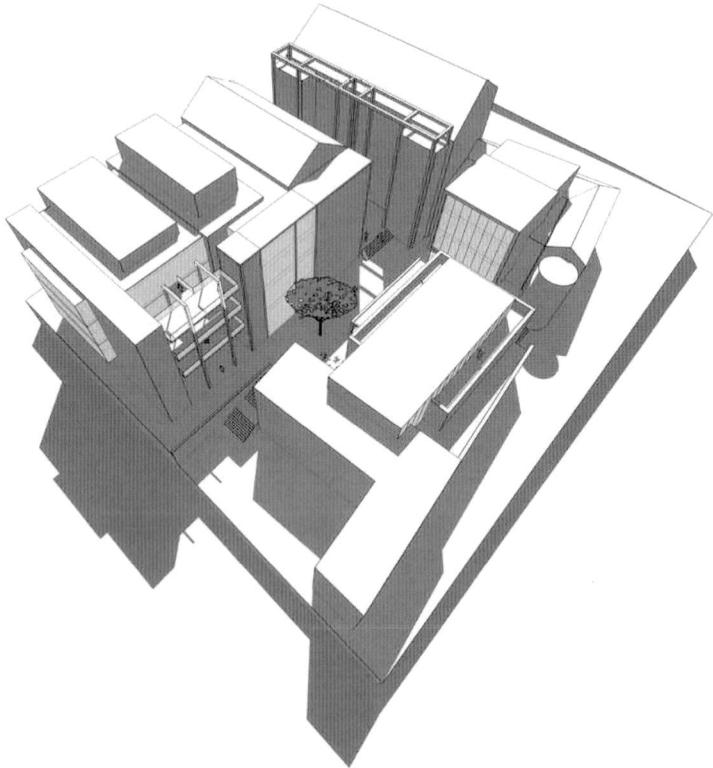

jayco house a project for 104 apartments in leeds for morris properties. the building is enclosed by a innovative vertical garden feature acting as a screen between apartments and neighbouring developments shared by other schemes in this city block. the garden theme is carried through the design with all apartments having individual winter gardens. the project has been submitted for planning approval - expected start on site - autumn 2006

great george street originally a masterplanning exercise for urban splash on a major liverpool location opposite to giles gilbert scott's anglican cathedral, the shedkm approach gained them preferred developer status and is now being progressed as a first phase. the design provides 250 starter home apartments using a similar plan form to moho manchester. currently the scheme is targeted at a march 2005 planning permission with further applications following suit

walsall parking hedge this concept (which has now been accepted as part of will alsop's masterplan) is currently being submitted for planning approval. the scheme uses an 850 space carpark as a 'green' screen to this canalside site which includes the caruso st john walsall art gallery and another shedkm scheme for a new HQ for the walsall housing group. the parking is screened in itself by a wall of planting and also accommodates a 120 room hotel

roscoe lane a liverpool project for ulster developer ashley moore, the project provides 370 car parking spaces in a multi storey building with 54 residential town houses and apartments set around a communal roof garden. the location is adjacent to rodney street which houses liverpool's main medical community, and is currently in negotiation with the city planning team. the concept of housing over an above ground carpark is new to liverpool - but has obvious potential

lister mills carpark part of the shedkm masterplan which is currently on site, the carpark also provides a major landscape at ground level with items such as natural ventilation inlets being designed as industrial scale sculptural objects. the lower carpark uses smooth white concrete with steel drum rooflights, and the entrance is marked by substantial steel portals and a corten boundary wall. the landscape is formal with podium steps and panels of white beach stones shedkm 1997 - 2005

people

james weston
jon falkingham
dave king
mark sidebotham
ian killick
hazel rounding
neil dawson
alan ross
lee halligan
nick birch
mark braund
helga steenweg wallin
quentin keohane
miles pearson
amanda wanner
gareth bansor
alex flint
bianka schmitt
alex williams
martyn thomas
carrie balmer
simon king
joshua williams
anna pavlova
ulrike schwickerath
beverly sanderson
dominic wilkinson
joerg schulte-wien
jean gors

photographs

lee halligan
jonathan keenan
hazel rounding
james weston
urban splash
dave king
ian killick
nick hufton
chris brink
phil sayer
shaw & shaw
martine hamilton knight

thanks to

nick bentley & uniform
paul sullivan & static
james clarke - brabners
malcolm grant - kemp & co
stewart barker - G & A
ian mcmurray & george day
matt wardle - black & ginger
miriam mezcua & ruth moreta
sarah humphreys
roger beysatt - apple
sophie king o'neill
keith rush & C3
pg displays
mike jones

'if there is a miracle in the idea of life, it is this - we are able to exist for a time in defiance of chaos....'

binyavanga wainaina